A Letter to My Son

written by:

Eric R. Robert

illustrated by:
Hatice Bayramoglu

This book is dedicated to my son Elijah R. Robert and all the fatherless sons in the world.

To my son, whom I love deeply I am writing this letter to you because I see the anger, pain, confusion and heartbreak in your eyes and in your actions.

I am writing so you don't become bitter, doubt yourself, your gifts or your talents. Son, allow this letter to give you clarity and understanding on what is happening around you. Most importantly, allow this book to shed light on who you are.

This letter will strengthen your faith, help you with your identity, and give you all the tools you need to be successful in this life and after. Son, this letter is your inheritance.

Dear Son,

Life is full of surprises and you can never control what happens but you can control who you are in the process of life. Life is based on principles and laws.

First, I want to talk to you about what you believe. My son, faith in God should be the foundation of any man. Who or what you fear determines your limitations. Fear no man, except God because in that fear or respect you find wisdom.

My son, wisdom is a principle defined as having experience with something, using good judgment or common sense.

When you rise daily seek God. Acknowledge God daily in all your ways. Ask these things of Him daily and you will be successful. Ask God for wisdom, knowledge, understanding and His revelation.

In receiving these things, you will have answers to every question pertaining to this life and thereafter. The beginning of wisdom is fear (reverence or respect) of God.

To have knowledge, means you have facts, information and skills that you've gained through experience or education. You must study but most importantly know what question to ask to get the answer you're seeking. Wisdom and knowledge cannot part ways from understanding. My son, you must possess understanding, which means to comprehend or know the meaning of what you ask for.

Your last task is to seek God's revelation. There are unknown facts about yourself and this world that you live in. This letter starts with you. Be the change you want to see within your family, friends and the people you will meet along the way. Read my letter daily. You may not understand things that are happening around you so let me help you.

The reason why there is crime, war, hatred, racism, murder, conflict, and divorce is because you don't ask of God who gives us liberally but when you do ask it's for your own pleasure not His glory. This means the only reason you want something is because someone else has it. Not because you want it to help or bring about a change or advancement.

Purpose for life

My son, this brings me to my second principle - do not walk in pride. Pride always comes before destruction. Pride is a need for help and thinking that it is not needed. Pride is self-willed. To be self-motivated and self-willed is different. The difference is one knows when to ask for help. The other thinks he can do everything without people or the help of God. This person you will not become. You must learn to forgive quickly because it prevents you from becoming bitter at people and life. Forgiveness is not forgetting, it is a choice to not hold a person's past against him/her. Forgive and learn of the offense and don't let it be repeated.

<u>Slow to speak and</u>
<u>quick to listen</u>

The third principle I have to teach you is correction. Always remember that correction is love. I guide you into the steps that will make life easier. Take my correction son, take my words and embrace them. Learn of all my mistakes and don't repeat what I have done. I will guide you on how to choose a wife, but before you choose a wife you must first know who you are and who you are not.

You must have character which is the true you when no one else is around. This is the person you live with daily. You must also have integrity, that is doing the right thing when it seems everyone else is doing wrong. Know your morals and have values, don't let anyone prevent or sway you from doing good to and for others.

Having morals and values are the codes of doing right, these are principles that you live by. This is also a quality you will look for in your spouse. Your spouse should have the same morals and values as you. Don't just look for beauty which is good, but what's better are the things of value hidden within.

You are A King

You must remember you are a protector, provider, promoter, a Priest/King, and prophet. A protector keeps everyone in their care safe emotionally, physically and mentally from things they can see and things they can't see. A provider handles all needs of those in your care, a provider is a giver not just in money but in counsel, friendship and many other areas that require you to give of yourself. A promoter lifts up your family, celebrates them and tells them daily who they are.

As a Priest, you hear from God and cast vision for the family, but this only comes by having a prayer life. As a King, lead by example and hold true to who you are, judge matters with your head and heart but judge matters fairly and justly with no bias.

As a Prophet, always speak the truth and stay away from lies. Please remember words affect life outcomes, this means what you say carries power and how you say it determines how it is heard.

Finding a wife

Now choosing a wife should come easy. Son, when you find her you will know. Just in case you don't know, here is what you should look for. She must first fear God and love Him above all things and submit to Him. Her actions must always align with what she says she believes. Make sure she is not quick-tempered or bitter from her past. She must be willing to submit to you and follow you as long as you are following God. She must be a servant to her family and a good homemaker but that doesn't mean she doesn't work. It means her family being taken care of is her top priority.

It is your responsibility to make sure her needs are met. She is a giver and a good manager of what's in her care. She makes wise decisions in her dealings with others, watch how she handles situations that she is faced with. She must make her choices based on the future not the present that means she plans ahead. She is to be a respectable, modest in her appearance and a skilled friend. Don't just look for the outward beauty which is good but look for the inward beauty that lasts far longer and will have a greater impact on your life and your children. Her morals and values must align with yours. My son remember when you find her you will receive favor from the Lord. That favor will help to ensure you are able to meet her needs. My son these are the components of a strong, healthy relationship.

1. **Communication**: How you talk to one another verbal and non-verbal is key. Do your best to be open and honest about your thoughts and feelings, and speak with love. Be patient in your conversations - listening with the intent of understanding.

2. **Mutual Respect**: Value the unique qualities that make them who they are.

3. **Trust**: Always have confidence that she will do the right things.

4. **Acceptance**: The moment you marry her let her past be the past.

5. **Shared Interest and Values**: Make sure you are going in the same directions in life and have common goals.

<u>Friendships</u>

My son, be wise watch how you pick your friends. Friends must not be violent or speak evil towards others - if they do you will soon find yourself doing the same thing. Watch the patterns of your friends because what they do you will find yourself doing or becoming associated with. So, in choosing friends take your time and know who they are when no one is around. Listen to their conversations and watch their actions so you will know exactly who they are.

Finances

My son, you ask why people are poor, it's simple, choice, chance and unfair circumstances. Work hard and stay focused on your gifts and talents and maximize yourself. Lazy people talk and dream. Talking and dreaming is good and it has its proper place. Dreaming helps you see past where you are and helps you create more than what you see. Self-talk can help push you through tough situations that you may face. Don't just talk and dream my son, execute on all you set out to do and you can do the impossible. Always have a plan and write down exactly what it is you want to see happen in your life and how you are going to achieve it with practical steps. When you receive money, you must know what to do with it. Try not to owe anyone money, if you do pay them back quickly. That's how you become trustworthy. Do not, I repeat do not co-sign for anyone. If you do be prepared to own the debt you signed for.

Always have a budget for the money you make in order to manage it properly. 100% of the money you make should be budgeted: take 10% and give it to church or a charity. Take 3% of every $1 you make and give it to yourself so that you can continue to develop yourself and your talents. Save 10% of all you make and finally, always live within your means. Money is a tool not the answer. Use money to create more tools or streams of income to build wealth. Invest only in what you understand, and think long-term because one day you will live off the investments you made in your earlier years.

To owe no man is the way you should live son, be debt free. To do this it will take discipline and a plan. It's okay to be rich and wealthy, my desire is for you to be rich and successful. Even more I want you to leave an inheritance for your children. Enjoy your life with balance, spend a little on yourself and be a good steward with all you have because if you are faithful with a little you will receive much more. Son, what you believe about money will affect your behaviors. It will cause you to make decisions and take actions in your own life. What you believe will determine your views on this matter so remember, money is a tool - don't love it but use it.

Trials of life: Adapt and Overcome

My son learn to overcome all challenges. Life can seem unfair but you have to learn to have faith in all things and have a vision to see beyond where you are today. Remember my words, seasons will change and people all over the world experience the same challenges but it's the people that have faith, hope, and love. No matter where you are today, you can always change for the better. Let the past be the past, learn from it, accept whatever happened and move forward. This is called hope and the end will result in joy and happiness if you finish your race. Love helps you to overcome all things, so love without limits. It's okay to be angry but don't let anger cause you to hate yourself or others. Let go of the things that hurt you, let go of situations you couldn't control and remember only you can control your actions.

Goal Setting

My son, you have the ability to adapt and overcome any challenge that sits before you. Don't forget you only have one body, so exercise daily and watch what you eat to live a healthy and strong life.

Now I must teach you how to set goals. Always remember anything you want in this life you must set goals to achieve. Each goal must be S.M.A.R.T.

The goal must be **specific** to what you want and very detailed. The goal must be **measurable** meaning you can track where you are and what's needed to get there and know when you've gotten there. It must be **achievable**, you must know that you can get there. **Relevant**: is the goal even worth it? Only you will know this. **Timebound**: when will I accomplish this goal?

My son setting goals in every area of your life such as spiritual, financial, career/business, family, health, relationship, personal growth and social will lead you to success but success means nothing without the right attitude. Having a positive attitude determines how high and how far you will go in life. This brings me to my last point.

Communication

Communication plays a major part in getting things done. How well you articulate your thoughts and ideas will help determine how many people you can lead and help. How you send verbal and nonverbal messages and receive a message is important for clarity and performance. My son, this letter is full of principles. If you read them daily and ask for understanding, you will find all the gems you need to be a great husband, father, friend and leader one day. You are great, you are a leader and not a follower. You are smart, good looking, and your generation needs what you have to offer.

There is so much more I want to teach you, but for now you have all you need to be all you are destined to be. Finally, know your surroundings, know your environment and be smart knowing that everyone doesn't have the same morals and values as you. Know that everyone doesn't fear God or see life as you do. Know that everyone does not seek peace. My son, know when to fight and when to walk away. Always stand for what's right, and remember those who are weak. Train to be strong spiritually, mentally, and physically. Spiritually through prayer daily, mentally through reading and feeding your mind with positivity. Physically learn to protect yourself, be skilled and peaceful. Don't take bribes and don't use drugs or anything that alters the mind. Put forth effort in all you do and keep your mind steady and be unified with your brothers always.

I love you son, and I am proud of you. I am thankful to be your father, I am also thankful for you.

Peace, mercy and grace be with you always.

Yours truly,
Dad.

P.S. Now I have to go talk to your sister. To be continued...

<u>About the Author:</u>

Eric R. Robert is a husband, father, educator, inspirational speaker, coach, and mentor to hundreds of individuals. Eric is from Marrero, Louisiana. He is married to Fatemah R. Robert, and they have one son together Elijah R. Robert. Eric is a graduate of Nicholls State University and holds a Bachelor in Liberal Arts. He holds two M.S. degrees, one in biblical studies from Friends International along with a Masters of Theology from St. John Bible Institute. He is the co-founder of 2randomguys, a coaching and consulting company in the area of helping people maximize their potential and reach their overall goals. He is currently working as the CFO at Children's Charter School in Baton Rouge, Louisiana.

For booking and/or speaking engagements you can contact me at <u>ericrobert24@yahoo.com</u>.

50583730R00015

Made in the USA
Columbia, SC
08 February 2019